AF269311

CENTRAL
TO
THE TASK

Saint Julian Press

Poetry

Praise for CENTRAL TO THE TASK

Lisa Rhoades is a wise guide through the physical landscapes of gardens and fields, as well as the equally brambly terrain of the heart. In both free verse and form, (pantoums, linked sonnets) Rhoades's deep engagement with the world allows personal experience to intertwine with larger themes. A loved one's cancer is compared to January 6th rioters, and an unsparing look at loss contrasts with appreciation for available grace. "Sometimes hands are meant to be empty," she tells us, yet also notes forsythia "unwinding/ the winter into an aura/of yellow-throated/stars." These are poems to savor.

Alison Stone
Author of *Informed* and *To See What Rises*

Reading the poems in Lisa Rhoades's new collection, *Central to the Task,* is like listening to the birds still in their trees before dawn. We can hear the birds' crescendos at inception. Sometimes ethereal and most often tangible, each poem is like a song reaching for and from grief, for and from solace, all the while grounding us: in queen Anne's lace and forsythia, noisy and fluttering birds, a "husband, kids, cats and dog." *Central to the Task* examines the loss that comes with living while reminding us how much beauty surrounds us and how possible recovery can be. These poems that Rhoades gives to us are, quite simply, prayers.

Deanna Benjamin
Co-Editor of *Narratives of Hope and Despair*
Ruin and Regeneration in Literature and Culture

Caught in the heart from the very first line—is what happens to the reader of Lisa Rhoades's new collection, *Central to the Task*. "Always some part of me standing at the shoulder,/ always/some part of me caught/longing/beside ditch flowers as they bob and nod." Rhoades's unique voice is soft, yet unsparing of truths: The heart is a "pile of briquettes waiting for a match." The smallest element of the natural world is a microcosm of daily life that inevitably explodes into a universe—which turns out to be the human heart, after all. "God at the lake honks like a goose..../....God being water/and the kayak, too." Her vocal control can be devastating. In "Texas Officials Incorrectly Claim a Teacher Left a Door Propped Open, Uvalde 2022" she offers her rage almost as prayer. "As if it was her fault, as if it was the rock's." When she uses form, she does so deftly. In "Samhain Pantoum": "I think this will be the year/I mark the thinning veil/without it gutting me./My dead will visit and leave." One is left struck by a sense of the totality of beauty in this work—the depth of feeling, the command of talent, the excellence of the art. For this reader, every poem is touching; the whole, a deeply satisfying read.

Michael Carman
Author of *The Not* and *You in Translation*

Throughout *Central to the Task*, Lisa Rhoades excels at the essential task of the poet—to pay close attention. Part urban pastoral, part domestic sublime, these subtle meditations seem generated directly from the grasses, the garden, and all the "weedy splendor" in the margins. As she seeks the precarious balance between the *green* and *not-green*, between spring and grief, Rhoades discovers an organic and authentic holiness, which feels as hard-won as it is greatly needed.

Jeanne Beaumont
Author of *Lessons with Scissors* and *Letters from Limbo*

CENTRAL
TO
THE TASK

Poems

Lisa Rhoades

SAINT JULIAN PRESS
HOUSTON

Published by
SAINT JULIAN PRESS, Inc.
2053 Cortlandt, Suite 200
Houston, Texas 77008

www.saintjulianpress.com

ISBN-13: 978-1-955194-49-5
Library of Congress Control Number: 2026930700

Cover Art: Elli Tzalopoulou Barnstone
Author Photo: Bonnie Nygard
Cover Design: Laura Smyth

For My Family, Always

CONTENTS

CENTRAL TO THE TASK

NOTES

ACKNOWLEDGMENTS

ABOUT THE AUTHOR

THE GRASSES OF THE FIELD

THE GRASSES OF THE FIELD

Always some part of me standing at the shoulder,
always
some part of me caught

longing
beside ditch flowers as they bob and nod
in the breeze kicked up by passing cars.

Chicory, day lilies and queen Anne's lace—
the grasses of the field

always a marvel, left to their business,
just out of reach of
the mower's blade.

Always this restless loss
as loosestrife and ragweed give way

to the yarrow's yellow buttons
unkept, unkempt beside a sloping field,

a graveled drive,
a few head of cattle, a swayback mare

some part of me
forever
a chigger bitten child

naming the barn cat's mewling litter,
naming what I cannot keep.

DRIFT

I can't see from this distance
what has gained the jay's attention,
but I understand his need—
it sends him hopping
from the ground to a branch
that gives and sways with his weight
as he wipes his beak by his feet,
drops out of view, and starts again.

Every day, the inexplicable—
the generosity of hydrangea,
blossoms made from clusters,
floret upon floret
all of them mounding
extravagantly to the ground.
Every day *green* in answer to the *not-green,*
the purple of the leaf's ribs
shining light against the body.

In any season, the suspension bridge
necklaces the bay, shore to shore,
the bridge itself
wearing a jewel tone stream of cars,
each with its humans, each
full of dreams.

Each with their worrying, too—
the sharp edges ground down,
gums scraped and oozing.
Dog with a bone. Cancer
halted in its tracks, but
also, sometimes, love.

Sometimes the work of flight is drift.
Sometimes hands are meant to be empty,
bones resting in their nest. The jay
will sometimes mimic a hawk's mew
to send the small birds spinning away in fear,
to have a little time at the feeder alone.

TO BE CLEAR

To be clear, it is less
that you thought it wouldn't happen—
you know the world has rhythms
and plans you can't see
or seeing can't understand,
like the time you tore out
that gangly thick-stalked plant beside the stairs
which wasn't what you thought
(a weed), but Asters,
and so denied yourself and the pollinators
a little sweetness before the cold,
only to have them come back the next fall,
your actions undone
and you happy for that in the end;

or that you don't have your own
ways of accounting for time, though
truthfully, they mostly center on your body,
the balance of accretions: what is lost,
what is gained, those muscles twinging
and all that gray;

after all, you've missed it up til now
so it's not that you thought it wouldn't happen,
so much as felt
it would happen without you,
like so much does,
while you're washing dishes
eyes lowered to the spot that needs extra soap,
not looking up, not noticing
the common yellowthroats and ovenbirds
migrating through your yard—
and when it rains tomorrow you'll remember

they move before a storm front,
fantastic creatures, skulking in the leaves,
in the tight lace of branches
you also meant to clear.

OF COURSE IT HURTS,

the heart,
with its cache
of unspent wonder,
that pile of briquettes
waiting for a match,
needing a flame.
Take for example
the hoof marks of deer
their "V" shape echoing
the geese above
while you remain tethered.
Someone keeps lining
the path through the woods,
shaping that dirt ribbon shining up
through the leaves,
with downed limbs
laid carefully end to end,
a sincerity of purpose
you scuff with your boot's edge,
traipsing along
through all this making
around you,
you with your hands tucked
into your pockets,
in a low blanket of fog
that wants to become rain.

ALMOST HOME

Mile over mile, henbit
tints the fields the interstate transects
past the Appalachians and through
the Susquehanna's central valley,
on the western plateau
where everything flattens toward Ohio.

April's still-grey trees and stubborn grasses—
more tan than yellow, more
yellow than green—
the embankments marked
with carcasses in succession:
deer, raccoon, opossum, hawk,
a democratic list of deaths
in any vernacular.

Why are my expectations
always of rust and moths,
always of the door to a treasure
thrown wide, waiting to
be plundered, or worse, an attic filled—
as if love could be banked, as if joy
were a silo filled beside a barn?

Tracts of winter wheat
lush and iridescent, bird-throat green,
sun through a 7-up soda bottle green,
alternate with last fall's thatch,
the cut, but not tilled-under, stalks,
and henbit, that purple, glowing weed—
holding the soil against the wind,
holding the soil against the rain,
in useful loveliness, in weedy splendor.

THE DEEP BELL

Rebuke
Brown apples and a deer carcass in the ditch.
Every straightaway a chance to gain speed,
but there's no leaving here. This place is stitched
into my family's myth, a life of needs
sometimes not met. I can romanticize
the view, especially in fall when light
retreats and the harvest's already prised
from stubborn fields and the bales are wrapped tight,
or try to blame the landscape for my crimped
heart, crenulated as the milkweed pods
and spears of sumac and goldenrod glimpsed
outside my speeding car—or maybe God.
But I'm the one who left, who let it go.
The deep bell in my chest rebukes me so.

The Broken Thing
The deep bell in my chest rebukes me, so
I go still and gaze toward the tidal strait
where the oil tanks sprout like mushrooms and glow
milk-blue in the evening light. I can't debate
my home's here now and Newark's runway lights
guide me to ground. The street I live on ends
at the Kill van Kull's dark waters, the tight
passage to the sea that separates me
from the continent. The Palisades darken.
The wind picks up. The leaves swirl with the snow.
Whatever I plant, I tend—a bargain
I made without knowing the cost of growth
that isn't mine. What I might miss.
Or how how the broken thing in me would resist.

Unfurling
Right now the broken thing in me resists
like knotweed answering a gardener's tug,
snapping at the ground while the roots persist,
propagating from fragments with a smug
efficiency. It's a wet spring but I'm
not losing days I can't make up, not watching
seeds rot in sucking mud, I've got time
to divide perennials, fill matching
pots with annuals or decide to quit,
let a lawn crew mow it flat, and embrace
a life like all the rest. Once I tossed seeds
from the porch, a string of stars that took
off toward the street. What will come up this spring
What did I plant while I was unfurling?

The Weather
A woman unfurls, starts planting her yard,
dreams she'll feed others and let herself be fed,
but the weather of her heart makes this hard,
leaving a mess of spent bulbs and woody
shrubs needing to be cut back. Ampleness
evades her. The lilies her grandma called
Naked Ladies choke themselves with success
and stop blooming. If she could just let old
expectations go, sow wildflowers, leave weeds,
watch the mourning doves brood their second clutch
on her porch and turn her face to the breeze,
letting go of blame, regret, and rage—so much
she cleaves to—and trust something good remains
that she could plant, and tend, and start again.

EVERY DAY IT'S THE SAME

A doe with a radio collar stumbles
hooves against asphalt
into the woods where she blends
as wild things are meant to do
with leaves, trunks, branches, stems.

My dog, who is sweet but not smart
whines softly, but not at the doe.
He's waiting for his doggy friend
who bullies him into the brittle red
of dried knotweed stalks
each time they run unleashed.

Every day it's the same between them:
Devotion. Whimpering. Treats.
Every day I walk the same
neighborhood loop tethered to patterns
I'd do well to shake off. Every day
the trees since late summer have pushed
each leaf cell by cell from its stem,
and the doe daily pings her location
to someone somewhere keeping track.

FAIRLY COMMON

On the pond this morning,
two hooded mergansers—male and female—
circle among the mallards
who also have returned. Praise the fancy
but fairly common, the male tuxedoed
in black and white, the female sporting
her cinnamon crest; their ducklings
flinging themselves like corsages
from tree cavity nests when just a day old.
Praise the estate planners two centuries ago
who excavated the clearing
and dammed up the spring;
and the generation who gave it all
to Children's Aid, who meant well
when they brought city kids
to its banks to play, snapping turtles
dropping into the mystery of their dreams.
Glory be to those who let it fall hushed
and overgrown. Praise the break in the
iron fence and the veil of forsythia
that hides it, and the locals
ignoring the *No Trespass* signs,
until a drunken teen missed the curve
and took two panels of fencing down,
praise the parks department
who let the gap remain.

SICK AT HEART

Saint Roch's dog
leans into his thigh,
offers up
a piece of bread, a bun
he's carried through the woods
on the scent
of the plague-sickened man.
Good dog.

Saint of the plague, of
doctors and dogs,
he pulls his coat aside
so viewers can see the buboe
on his leg, the freakish wounds
of his martyrdom,
and dark memento mori clouds—
details meant to soothe
those who can read signs.

Quiet as a fawn, my dog
licks his paw, soothed
by the warm drag of his tongue
across his pad,
he keeps at it until it's raw.
It was a mistake
to bring him home
when I was so sick at heart,
a mistake
to think we could give each other
what we need:

that I could cup the kibble
in my hand, saying
here is food, it is safe to eat,
frustration excised from my voice;
that he could rest his head
against me as we sit,
and wellness would spring
between us, and we would
leave our wounds alone—
maybe heal, maybe stop
limping along.

GINNY IN JUNE

loves dandelions and stands
with an open globe,
and then blows and shrieks
and looks for the next. In the ball field
where we let the dogs run,
the grasses have gone to seed,
the baseball diamond is un-raked, the basketball
hoops removed, so that kids in quarantine
won't try to play, won't yell
and shout and jump this spring.
She won't remember this. She won't
remember how we held our breath.
The broad leaf plantain nods
its swollen bud, bindweed twists
through the chain links, a constellation of pink
clover swirls through the smaller white.
She picks flowers one by one.
She sends them flying
on the path of her breath.

GOD AT THE LAKE

God at the lake honks like a goose
like all of them thwacking the surface, lifting to flight
or lazing one-legged on the floating dock
preening the feathers across their backs, shaking
their heads, tucking their bills to their breasts. God
the heron watches, feet in brown sand
as God the minnow flits
shadow to shadow. God the teenage lifeguard says
it's not a bad first job, spading over moats and gullies
God the toddler made before this tantrum—
too tired to nap, too desperate to stay—
God tips over the canvas tote bag and cries.
God the sand fly burrows and burrows
and doesn't sting or bite.
God the red-eared slider suns on the stump
ignoring the kayaker,
the kayak hissing through the water grasses
God being water
and the kayak, too.
God the sunny nibbles at the worm
who is also God and so suffers this attention.
God the lure, the hook, the floater, the sinker,
and the boy learning to cast a line,
God aiming toward God,
the tilting buoy in the center of the lake.

PROVIDENCE

This is a poem about growing older,
a poem about visiting my hometown
and yes, finding many things changed.
My own body, for example,
cradling the muscle memory of location,
gets distracted by roads widened
or re-routed completely—Green Meadows for one,
now ends in a cul de sac instead of trailing off
into the gravel road we called the seven hills.
The last mile of the bus route our pack of kids—
the Walters and Coxes, the Rhoadeses and Walls—
would move to the back and bounce as the bus crested
each hill to make ourselves, just for a moment, fly.
When I came down hard on the seat's metal frame
and got the wind knocked out of me,
John the driver thumped my back,
and made everyone ride forward the rest of the year.

I was still in high school when Providence
was extended, and the bluff was blasted
into a bright limestone cliff.
The cell phone tower that breaks the horizon,
arms equal in length and wrapped
in fake evergreen, came more recently.
Why do they try to camouflage them like that?
Who looks up and mistakes the tower for a tree?
Who else besides me remembers the maple
that stood there for years, catching
the morning light in early fall, blazing gold to red
on this road named for the protective care of God?

FIVE QUESTIONS

On the Cornell Ornithology website
I answer five questions to find
that the bird flitting above my neighborhood pond
is an American Redstart who, despite the name,
is black with orange on its sides, wings and tail.

My daughter had said, "if anyone can
identify that bird it's you," even though
that's not how I feel, even though I have reached
the margins of my mothering, handing my kids
to therapy and their friends, those staircases
away from their father and me.

They've never seen the drawers in museums—
each species labeled with its genus, each family
in its class, all the wingspans pinned open
or closed, the sunken eye sockets,
the taxidermied hearts.

When we get home I make a pot of tea, twisting
orange peel into the pot, watching the rind
float briefly and sink. The morning's details
fan out in brilliant flashes. My kid
believes I will get it right.

CANOPY AND CROWN

Oh Red Oak, dear straight and massively branched tree,
crown of glory, crown of the corner of Prospect
and Lafayette, perhaps of the entire Staten Island North
Shore, a *planting of the Lord*, ancient shelterer
of heucheras and hostas, of many
tender perennials, of small creatures and birds, filtering
winter sun to the faces of Lenten roses, offering shade
from late spring to autumn,
to generations, not only my own, of friends
(so many dead or otherwise gone)
and babies crawling across small quilts in its cool.
The ground below it holds the ashes
of several beloved pets and once revealed
a porcelain doll head, the doll's soft body gone
while the tree grew on, each fall replenishing
the soil with itself, decay feeding
every plant beneath its canopy.
The trunk filled the view from the kitchen door
with rough rivers of bark running foot to sky.
What once was a tender shoot, a root out of dry ground,
it grew each year until it couldn't, building out
from its heartwood ring upon ring.
Grey fungus blossoms on its upper bole
and large branches signaled its distress,
so did acorns in abundance.
"Hazard" and "limb drop," "die back" and "shatter"
poured into our conversations.
So sky entered where there once was a tree
and the shade loving plants ached under the sun,
as we listened to the wood chipper grind away
at that which had lifted up branches
in faithfulness to the sky.

THE ANTHOLOGY
OF UNASKED FOR PLANS

THE ANTHOLOGY OF UNASKED FOR PLANS

In the Anthology of Unasked for Plans,
filed under Cancer, subsection: not mine,
I have to put my father-in-law
standing at a window in mid winter,
unwilling to consider the country of wounds
to which his body has already
purchased its ticket.
He cancels what he can:
the second opinion, the limo set up
to get him there, his wife who wants
to sit and hold his hand,
even the phone call with his sons
that was meant to follow, their grasping for
options, their desperate love.

In the kitchen the TV is tuned to the news:
where a mob has stormed the Capitol
propelling leaders to their knees—
a loop he half listens to. "Jackasses" he says
and the word feels good, feels warm as it moves
through his mouth, so he says it again:
"jackasses" this time meaning the surgeons,
perhaps even his sons, as much as the mob
smearing their feces on the walls.
Or maybe he means his own body:
the spectacular failure his organs are arranging,
his pancreas leading the way,
wearing its plum-veined scarf of tumor,
terrorist desecrating everything within reach.

THEY'VE DECIDED WE'RE NOT IN THE
ANTHROPOCENE—

Our mid-20th century blanket
of plutonium over everything–
ocean bottoms to muddy riverbanks–
our heavy metals, asphalt and trash,
fertilizers, and industrial ash
mark something, but not an epoch we get
to name. We're stuck in the late Holocene
stumbling toward the sixth great extinction
fattened with our microplastics. We'll leave
a time plane of chicken bones and concrete,
everything we crushed to make everything
we made. No surface trace of what we loved
or of the names we've given to our pain.

PRUNING THE BITTERSWEET

Dear friend, this morning I opened the front door
to find a small dead bird on the welcome mat,
lying on its side, unbloodied, just still,
probably from a quick smash
against the beveled glass. It wasn't a sparrow,
but was sparrow-sized, and brown
with black stipples on its tail.
I carried it to the farthest corner of the yard
and dropped it into composting leaves.

It's three days shy of the anniversary of your death,
which is to say, just a Tuesday in July,
not the day itself, or the day I learned the news,
or the day we lifted your memory to God,
but maybe the one on which we met
in the hallway at church
and you reminded me of your upcoming trip,
and I told you we would miss you
at the baseball game.

So I mark the morning as I do most days,
with a list of tasks that must get done.
I start early with weeding the garden beds, pruning
the bittersweet by the fence, dragging the reaching
tendrils from where they've caught
in the magnolia branches,
and pulling them from the dirt
where they've reached back to send up suckers
throughout the yard.

CARDINAL

My nephew says seeing a cardinal means
there's a soul nearby, so I wonder who's flitting
from the red oak to the neighbor's fence
to watch us at this vacation house.

I hope it doesn't need to be
someone recently dead,
because my grandmother would love the view
of her greats—cavorting from lawn to dock,
diving and jumping into sun-warmed shallows,
shrieking as their toes sweep the silty bottom.

But it's ok if it's my friend
whose recent death has hinged
my middle age, the counting-ness
that entered with that grief—
zero, one, two, three—
the natural set of losses into which he fit,
and just like that. *Cardo, Cardinis, Cardinal,*
the heart pivots, the count goes on
though not every death or number
works that way.

We spend most of our week here
out on the boat, dragging the kids
on a giant inflatable raft
that skids back and forth across our wake.
No cardinal mark warns us from the channel's
hidden sandbars so we find
safe waters on our own.

Our New World songbird got its name
from Old World scarlet robes, or so the internet says.
Also, "cardinals appear when angels are near"
can be engraved, embossed or stitched
onto the tchotchke of your choice,
which explains my nephew's solemn assertion.
The red flash by the sliding glass doors
fights his reflection in defense
of a cup of twigs lined with soft grasses and hair.
Poor soul.

WHAT DO YOU NEED?

Do you need me to turn my back,
go for a cup of coffee in the cafeteria,
rustle around a few extra minutes
searching for sugar or cream,
or turn down the wrong corridor or better still
walk past your quiet room?

Should I let my head nod over this puzzle
or watch a little TV? I wish I could
turn it over to the professionals,
or take the means into my hands:
gird myself against your wince
at what is small and bitter
and hard to swallow, against your gasp
which turns into a small coo,
which makes it seem as if
you are becoming a small bird
but is just air passing over vocal cords.

TEXAS OFFICIALS INCORRECTLY CLAIM
A TEACHER LEFT A DOOR PROPPED OPEN,
UVALDE, 2022

And that's how the shooter got in.
As if it were her fault, as if it were the rock's—
tumbled smooth along the river bed
or sharp as flint, fissured and cracked,
coughed up from when this place was a sea, flecked
with quartz, flecked with small round fossils,
little crinoid buttons chipped free
and set on a shelf beside other precious things,
or sheared from a mountaintop, crushed by machines
and left beside a door. Perhaps it was
the noonday heat, the cool breeze
up from the water, or rustling through
the blooming trees, moving toward the building,
summer almost here flooding the hallway
the cross draft from a window lifting
the edges of the papers, sweeping across the desks
and the small warm bodies in their chairs.

NOT THE HAWK

When I reach to cup my hand
to the back of my son's head,
and some weight of him
rests again in me,
this boy whose body poured
from mine
one deep December night,
I am not the hectoring jay
not the squirrel wasting seeds,
or garter snake mid-road
and crushed, blood and tissue
dry as leaves, not the dog barking
against its chain,
nor the snapping turtle,
waiting in the mud.
I am briefly not the hawk
catching the updraft,
circling,
until the small birds cry
and spin away.

SPRING BREAK

The daughter, alone in a room, burns
incense, its thick scent hanging.
The mother drifts outside the girl's door
the whole of the cold spring day.

Incense, a thick scent. Hanging
over them: "she" is now "they."
The whole of the cold spring day
the mother absorbs this change.

Around them ("she" is now "they")
the world explodes in leafy joy.
The mother absorbs this. "It changes
nothing," she whispers. "I see your multitudes."

The world explodes. In leafy joy
the mother drifts. Outside the girl's door:
nothing. She whispers, "I see your multitudes."
The daughter, alone in a room, burns.

BAD OCEAN

Years ago, at the beach my child and a friend
scolded the waves as they crashed to the sand,
running at the water's edge like those birds,
sandpipers perhaps, or black-necklaced plovers,

laughing and screaming, "Bad ocean! Bad!"
because of the accident they'd witnessed
the day before when their dad was flung headfirst
by the tide and broke his humerus at its neck

and stumbled toward them cradling himself
as he once had held them, but now
an adult in pain—the first they'd seen—
but of course, not the last.

SEMBLANCE

The sunchokes lean and crowd in the corner
of the yard, the teenage girls of my autumn garden,
shy in their height and prickly armed, a joyous yellow
that seems planned to bridge from August's wilt to fall
if you didn't know their tubers kill tender perennials.

Some days I get caught up in the happy semblance:
flowers from the yard to fill a vase,
my grandmother's ice blue, smooth-lipped plates
set for our evening meal;
or husband, kids, cats and dog,
crowded onto my bed, our warm animal smell—

but the friend who gave me the rootlings
said, "be careful, they will spread"
and then stepped out of my life for good,
leaving me on my knees to curse and tear
through more than one summer day;

and my grandmother taught me
to candle incubating eggs—shine a too-bright light
through each milky shell,
confirming the life fluttering on the other side—
because "yolkies," "quitters" and "winners"
look the same to the naked eye
but some of them are ready to explode.

"ONE OF THESE THINGS IS NOT LIKE THE OTHERS"

"One of these things just doesn't belong,"
goes the Sesame Street song—
an early lesson in sorting by difference:
a cow, a bird, a plane and a bee
play across the television screen.
Which one will you pick, the one not alive
or maybe the one without wings?
You know the circle in Duck, Duck, Goose
will shift itself closed when you stand—
another lesson you've already learned:
outside versus in. One dad has cancer,
one dad drinks, one dad has lost his job.
You know there's no prize
if they're all yours. You close your eyes
and wait for the tap on your head,
so you can unfold the pleat
of your knees to your chest,
take a deep breath, and run.

MIGRATORY

I stand in the parking lot beside the car
to watch geese arc their path
far overhead
before I click the lock
and the horn beeps back
and I step into Emergency
where we wait all night
as tragedies bigger than ours
come through the doors—
my meager heart and your
alcoholic fog technically not enough
to cause alarm, even though
they dissolve our family on touch.
Like the birds, 1 traveled here
by instinct, like the birds
it's also clear I'll come back
to pick you up when you're discharged
caught with you in a tightening loop,
unable to reach the altitude
I need to leave.

GRIEVANCE

Being lied to, I
lied. An illness
I carried. A sorrow,
a wound
reluctantly unwrapped—
the gauze of it dingy,
resisting the scissors,
my dull attempt
to cut.

The wrong of it, a pebble
doing the sharp work
of glass—
pressing insult.
And my body
responding—the heel
protesting first, a subtle
change of gait,
then the hip's new ache,
the poor sleep
it dogs me through—
the nightmares like clothes strewn
on a gravel shoulder:
socks and underclothes,
one black shoe.

And so it goes—
grit in the sponge. I walk
to work. My forehead
complains to the sun,
and the breeze leaves
salt crystals, trace
minerals, and all the rest.

ABOUT THOSE YEARS

I confess the whole
broken list, the bursts
of my rage, the bitter words
I laced us with; how I fell in love
with sleeping alone, curled
my flesh to my own flesh,
the dog pressed
at the back of my knees;
how I didn't leave,
but I didn't decide
to stay, and so turned
this little family
into an island wreathed
in sharks, no SOS writ large
across the wide beach, just me
keeping the fire
of my grievance lit,
feeding it, meting out
love like rice grains, like
the last clean water, while
I stayed wrapped
in my suffering
and the kids
did what they could,
the older teaching
the younger how to swim,
or at least how not to sink.

THREE CONFESSIONS

At the touch of my hand, the dog
sometimes flinches, though he sleeps
beside me nightly, and never leaves
my side. He deserves a better person,
one not quite so loud, who also needs
to stop and stand when trucks roar by.
If I could make it up to him I would,
with favorite foods and love-cupped hands.
I'd restore the storm-tossed nest we come across
to the safest spot I can find. I'd admit
how lucky his love makes me feel.
Confession #2: insert "husband"
where "dog" appears;
Confession #3: now, insert "child."

DETAILS I BURY

An Eastern Towhee showed up in the yard
scratching leaf litter for insects and seeds,
a dark hooded male with brick red flanks
and white breast, details I bury myself with today—
filling first my heart, and then the space
around my feet, a carpet of words like "hood,"
like "flank" instead of "constant" and "blame,"
instead of "please why can't we talk,"
or all the codes we have for leave me be,
all the ways two people can be lost
standing in their own backyard,
dragging a twig through the spring mud
a boundary the rummaging little birds will obscure.

SAMHAIN PANTOUM

I think this will be the year
I mark the thinning veil
without it gutting me.
My dead visit and leave.

I mark a thinning veil
of frost across the yard.
My dead visit and leave
while I garden, while I clean

the frosty yard
and mound the beds.
I garden. I clean.
I wait for it to end.

I mound the beds.
They look like graves.
I wait. For it to end
I know I have to let go.

My beds look like graves.
Without it gutting me,
I know I will let go.
I think this will be the year.

ON CANDLEMAS

I meet the winter's midpoint at the beach
looking to be healed—the dog's wounded paw,
and my heart leaning cruel—by the ocean's
salty lick, the simple prayers of shells and rocks.
I don't know what to make of the dead gull
laid out, breast up, on a piece of driftwood,
both the hammered gray of overcast skies,
except consider it an offering–
something done with gentle hands but odd, far
from the inky storyline the tide inscribes.
Beneath my feet the small shells crack and split.
I expect to leave unblessed, head tucked against
the wind and the dark days still ahead–
empty. I whistle the dog to my side.

CENTRAL TO THE TASK

CENTRAL TO THE TASK

Central to the task is the tambourine, shaking
and jangling its delight, despite
the clatter of your heart, that nervous castanet.

Central to the downpour is the view from the garage,
the water sheeting from the roof,
the misty look of the yard beyond.

Central to the tree, the rain stipples its surface, running
like a tendon or a braid,
a boundary drawn, the heartwood hidden.

Essential to the fields are grey silos at intervals,
the compass that can be made of a vertical line against
the horizon, the way home shining radium green
as headlights bounce off the mile markers.

And on the subject of lighting, the sconces in the living
room rebuke the dusk as it gathers, whispering
of cocktail parties and boulevards, distinguished guests
with perfect posture.

And on the subject of parlors, the pocket doors
nudge open because the dog has built his life
around the sound of your breathing,

And speaking of devotion, the mail provides
an envelope nestled in the catalogs, you touch
the familiar hand.

THE BIND

The yard fills with grackles–
from the neighbor's oak to my damp slope,
they swoop and chatter, drawn by something
cracked open, grass seeds or clover,
this early week of warm weather.
The older I get the more it seems
it's on me to decide what harbingers
to follow, to know which
are stepping stones to grief,
and which to Spring. The grass seethes
with iridescent noisy birds
weaving the news of abundance
through the trees, the new season
into the old, and I
want to keep my heart intact,
lace the dark into the light,
bind the habit of blessing both
to this life.

HISTORY OF LOVE

My first summer in Baton Rouge
I didn't have a job or friends,
I hadn't started school, I couldn't
stand the heat. Each afternoon
dark storm clouds roiled,
the sky turned a yellow bile
and rain would pound
the leaves and sharp-edged grasses,
then just as quickly stop.

Later in the buggy damp
a would-be lover tried
to seduce me on the levee,
above the river's flat black,
with the tower stacks of the refinery
spine-like on the far bank,
but I wouldn't undress
until we returned to the cool blast
of the window unit beside his bed.

I could drive to his bungalow
if I had to now, but I have lost
his name, not getting to pick
which memories keep
and which evaporate—
steam lifting from a rain-struck street,
as afternoon crawls.

WE'RE HERE

I apologize to the Aster, whose leaf I do not know
and so I treat it like a weed and rip it
from near the front porch stairs.
I am sorry, too, my first marriage failed
and with it my twenties and most of the next
decade as well. Living on the student side of town,
I bought a bike, and then a car.

I thought of that this morning
while riding the S94
turning onto the Terrace
across from Atlantic Salt
where a ship with a crane piled great clawfulls
of rock salt into a mountain several stories tall.
Because "Manitowoc" painted in white
across the red-black hull took me back
to a crummy apartment above 4 young guys,
who'd come from Manitowoc to Madison
to work and live a while.

That's how my brain works these days, traveling
back and forth, grief, to grief, to grief.
On the ferry I am forever
waking people when we've arrived, tapping
someone who's nodded off with a soft "we're here."
Those kids were nice to me
when I broke my leg that fall,
letting me sleep on their couch.

BODY WORK

Years ago, before a massage I'd tell
the therapist there's a good chance I'll cry
because my divorce now thirty years on
lives where the trapezius and rhomboid
overlap. A button when pushed that summons
my ex in youthful glory, me nearby,
both laid out like kids in snow, but on
an autumn bed of Gingko gold instead.
Why did we have a camera with us?
Who took the picture? Who processed the film?
I know when we split up I didn't ask
what she wanted, nor did I guess
that the memory of how it felt to be
possessed would travel so deep, and stick.

ACCOUNTING

I wish I did better counting blessings,
that my list would not be so spare, that I
could call the redbud on the corner
gemlike, without drawing your attention
to the side that's bare, the side I can't un-see,
the side that died when they re-poured the curb;
that I wouldn't want my house as quiet
and clean as the widow's next door: how she
reaches into and shrugs off the empty mailbox,
pansies hanging in planters from hooks on her eaves.
On my porch, the mourning doves
have returned to their nest and already
the first hatchlings are readying to leave—
a daring swoop to the power line, and then
to the rest of the world, leaving me
with a mess of twigs and shit to clean.

ESPALIER

If I could fix hope
to a trellis, I would tie
the branches
in the direction of love,
pruning what reaches away,
patient as someone
who expects to be around,
and the tree would answer
with dense blossoms
and the mouths of the blossoms
would fold into the fruit,
and the fruit would hang
in a pattern of great beauty,
and it would be enough,
it would feed the world.

ABIDING

And the spirit of the Lord pushed
a wheelchair up 3rd Avenue
and the chair held a plastic bin and several bags
and the spirit wore a cloud of gray hair, a sweatshirt
and bedroom slippers and moved so slowly—
half step, half shuffle, the right foot always leading
the left, as the countdown to the red light flashed
in gold—that the cars started to inch forward
but the spirit kept the pace,
didn't rush or even notice
that no one really wanted to wait
for the spirit abiding in our midst, poured
out before us, binding up
the brokenhearted, making a glorious name.

BREAKING THE FAST

My cab driver is breaking his fast—
chicken curry, lentils, puffed rice,
guava, sliced green apples,
and Jelebi, the sweet, nested
in containers on the front passenger seat—
"dry food" by which he means not heavy
or with too many vegetables
which might cramp his long-empty gut.
We say the things we say in cabs:
we are lucky for our families, our homes,
our jobs, we are grateful for God
and food, and while we are sharing,
he offers me a taste of his meal
and with it his wife's love, her knack
with spices and efficiency with knives.
He wants me to feel these blessings
which have traveled all day beside him
up and down the great Avenues
and the smaller streets where the tree pits
are filled with jonquils and the trees themselves
are blooming, even the branches
beneath the scaffolding,
through the midday cloud burst,
and the puddles at the curb cut
where the runoff didn't fully drain.

MEANWHILE, THE WORLD

Meanwhile the world
shimmers and shimmies around—
a constant weaving of insects and bees,
the warblers moving through
on their way further north,
all the perennials unfurled,
and the canopy of the maples complete—
not even a dapple
of light remains beneath.
In pots, heirloom tomatoes
started from seed
and gifted to me by a friend, wait
for their turn to go in the ground,
the lilac needs a hard prune,
the iris will open next week.
However high the neighboring plants,
the Star of Bethlehem sends its stalk
a little beyond so the flowers lift
their faces well into the sun,
as the chameleon plant stretches roots
sideways under the bluestone walk
no matter how often I weed it back.
Which is to say they make a path.
Which is to say they get it done.

THERE SHE GOES AGAIN

The purple iris closest to the house,
have bloomed this April 7th afternoon,
and before you think, *there she goes again,*
talking about her yard, when there's so much
more in even her small life deserving
her attention–her marriage perhaps,
or youngest child, the roof's now full-blown leak,
the brown stain it makes against the pale pink
in the hallway. Well, duh. What can she do
to change the story? The world sped up
without asking her, and now the iris
shoulder in before the jonquils undress,
spring racing through one April afternoon
a pattern she understands, just compressed.

THE VISIT

Two weeks ago the rains washed crickets
beneath the basement Bilco doors
bringing good fortune or foretelling death
depending on the source. Uncatchable,
though I have tried, wanting to drop them
into a flower bed, back into the world
where they belong, where they are meant
to lay eggs in the soil and die. Instead
they have made this house a field,
these chilly days, a summer night,
and I will be sad when they fall silent for good
not just each time I flick on the lights—
little hearts that keep playing their song,
that keep trying to find love here.

THRIFT

We don't get to choose
our portions of gladness
or how absolutely tied
they might be
to a childhood of wood smoke
late Sunday afternoons, drifting
from one back yard
to the next.

Neither what pains:
the heart's cellar,
with its soured butter beans
and mason jars tight with rust,
baling wire threading the knuckles
of the furnace hinge,
a spindle tightening everything to itself.

Is it a mistake
for the rose to spend
its single November bloom
as confetti for the grass, or
the towhees to stop their
scratch for insects and seeds
to sing and counter-sing?
Is it wrong to be satisfied
by what's been given,
by what's been given
made glad?

GOTCHA

Last night I was a tourist in my dream
unable to decipher the price tags
of sequined blouses I wanted to buy
for friends, being neither sparkly nor
diaphanous myself and feeling rushed
as shopkeepers closed the stores by folding
them shut like origami movie sets.
Time snaps a dishcloth against my thigh
saying "gotcha" and running from the room,
while we've squandered 13 cancer-free years
with our heads still down, as if this life
were something to get through, work to shoulder—
years that should have been a blessing, that were
a blessing, if only we'd looked up.

MAKING DO

What if the well-meaning
hand me downs
and perennials pinched
from someone else's yard
and healed into my own,
could mute sorrow
turn it into a balm,
turn it into an open ticket
a calligraphic promise
of something more,
something lustrous and dear?
After all, I traveled when I was young—
I've visited the sea, and wrapped myself
in blue silk against the evening chill;
and say what you want, it's a skill
making do—adding an extra cup
of water to the pot as the chicken carcass boils—
making just a little more broth, enough
for me to share, to bring to you, gold
and shimmering with the tiniest beads of fat,
yet nothing but water, bones and time.

SOME CARE

Does the lake always stream as if it's a river,
I ask my friend as we look out the window
of her dining room at the water beyond.
Her husband thinks the new dock is shoddy
and shows me with his hands how he'd dovetail
the joints while the wind keeps coming from the south
and pushing and puckering the evening light
until it stops. The water and sky flatten gray.
He asks me if I'm happy.
I ask him how happy does one have to be.
The dock is sturdy even if his eyes
stray to the gaps, and the untreated wood
will last with a coat of paint and some care.

STILL NECESSARY

All weekend a kernel of loss
nudged me along, October
does that sometimes, each morning
a little darker on the staircase
out of summer.
I am looking for mercies this Monday:
for my body to ache less,
for my marriage to feel
like purple Asters—sturdy and sweet
reaching out by the steps
a late gift to the bees—
instead of like a field sculpted by hurt,
seeded with a crop never meant
for summer feasts, not
Ambrosia, Nirvana, or Silver Queen
just dent corn, tough and stripped
from its stalks, scattered
in the combine's wake,
but still necessary, still food.

LANDMARKS

Even mown, the field shines gold,
grasses fanning up in a whorl—
reverse sunrays—pointing
to the overcast sky,
a halo hammered thin.

The field, the players,
the flattened baseline,
the ball sailing
to the wild edge of things—
all around you the world
makes itself right. The rose
continues its conversation
with the railing
you've lashed it to;
the black walnut spills
its fruit, a perfect gift
inside a bitter hull.

Even bruised,
your marriage plows on.
Why are you astonished
at the landmarks
you've been given:
the mulberry at the corner,
the dog's head upon your thigh,
the sparrows below the feeder
scratching for something more?

FORTUNE COOKIE

To *"embrace this love relationship you have,"*
I blur my sadness and double my joy–
in this retelling I never got sad,
you never got cancer, and my anger
never strained the anchor keeping us safe.
The electric blue of our love's harbor
never muddied, never failed to mirror
such absurd happiness our friends went mad
with envy. In this version we meander,
there is enough money to retire,
no aches to dissect, no glass half empty
or half full, just the steady kerplunk,
kerplunk of your heart against my hand,
my hand on your chest, our contented sighs.

IF NOT LOVE

> *"people during times of prolonged radical change,*
> *end up changing"* NYT, April, 2020

I was hoping for a softening—
an end to petty cruelties,
a reckoning that's just.
If not ease, at least the shovel
not always hitting stone—
the rocks arranged into a path,
the hold on my heart
loosened just a notch.
So my home becomes a refuge
my marriage a garden, my garden
a bower, lush and not overrun,
because if not peace
then oak, generous and branching,
each year the last to bud,
if not reprieve then the cherry
finishing its bloom, petals
like love letters to the gutters,
the grass. If not love
then sorrow withdrawn, assuaged,
if not blessing then the bumblebee
drunk in the tulip's cup.

THE FORSYTHIA

Edges everything–every highway
in spring, boundless, un-
bound, unwinding
the winter into an aura
of yellow-throated
stars, spilling
their brief
wild-twigged moment
before wicking green–spring
rendered, spring bending
into itself with daughter shoots
digging in where the fountains
meet the dirt, making of itself
a brake of yellow bells, what
blossoms without tending,
what blossoms when abandoned.
What blossoms.

ACKNOWLEDGMENTS

Thanks to the editors and staff at the journals and magazines in which the following poems appeared (or are forthcoming as of May, 2026) sometimes in different forms:

Amethyst: "Espalier" and "Samhain Pantoum,"
Boulevard: "Bad Ocean,"
Calyx: "Central to the Task" and "Spring Break,"
Cider Press Review, "Semblance,"
Common Ground Review: "Thrift" and "To be Clear,"
Hyacinth Review: "Gotcha,"
Literary Mama: "Not the Hawk,"
Louisville Review: "If Not Love,"
MockingHeart Review: "Texas Officials Incorrectly Claim a Teacher Left a Door Propped Open, Uvalde 2022,"
Nimrod International Journal: "Sick at Heart" and "What Do You Want?,"
Permafrost: "Still Necessary,"
Pirene's Fountain: "Forsythia," "They've Decided We're not in the Anthropocene," and "Three Confessions,"
The Poeming Pigeon: "The Visit,"
Poetry South: God at the Lake,
Quartet: "Providence,"
Rogue Agent: "Body Work,"
Rust and Moth: "Details I Bury,"
The Southern Review: "History of Love" and "Of Course It Hurts,"
SOFLOPOJO: "The Grasses of the Field,"
StoneBoat Journal: "Drift,"
SWWIM: "Ginny in June," "Pruning the Bittersweet," and "Landmarks,"
Thin Air: "Meanwhile, the World,"

Windhover: "The Deep Bell," and "Breaking the Fast,"
West Trestle: "Anthology of Unasked for Plans."

Thank you so very much to The Virginia Center for the Creative Arts and SWWIM—The Betsy South Beach for residencies where I could focus on these poems.

Deep gratitude to the writers in my online poetry groups, especially Celia Bland, Elizabeth Bruce, Debra Gregerman Joan Poole, Lindsey Royce and Agnes Vojta for inspiration and encouragement; to Jeanne Beaumont, Deanna Benjamin, Michael Carman, and Alison Stone for their generous words, and to Victoria Hallerman, Robin Locke Monda and Robert Monda for always offering wise critique.

Aliki Barnstone, Kathleen Crown, Catherine Doty, Caroline Hastie, Elizabeth Howell, Kelly Linn, Denise Stone, Blake Traylor, and Tracy Williams where would I be without you?

Elli Tzalopoulou Barnstone, your work and your memory are daily blessings in my life. Marybeth Rivera, thanks for your easy friendship. Laura Smyth you have my undying gratitude.

David, Bonnie and Charles, I love you.

Ollie, thanks for all of the W-A-L-K-S.

NOTES

The Grasses of the Field refers to the Bible verse Matthew 6:30.

Almost Home refers to the Bible verse Matthew 6:19-21.

Sick at Heart refers to the story of Saint Roch, a 14th century French Nobleman, who is the Patron Saint of plague victims and dogs.

Ginny In June is for Virginia Rivera.

God at the Lake is for Denise Stone.

Canopy and Crown refers to the Bible verses Psalm 36:5 and Isaiah 61:3.

The Anthology of Unasked for Plans references the January 6, 2021 storming of the United States Capitol by Trump supporters.

Pruning the Bittersweet is in memory of Charles Henry Howell.

A cardinal number is a type of number defined in such a way that any method of counting sets using it gives the same result. Thanks to Sam Williams for helping me with that math.

What do you need? is in memory of Mary Cunning and Delilah.

Semblance references the practice of candling eggs that are being incubated to see if they are viable.

Samhain Pantoum refers to one of the four Gaelic seasonal festivals including Imbolc, Bealtaine, and Lughnase and occurs halfway between the Autumnal Equinox and Winter Solstice.

On Candlemas refers to the celebration of the Feast of the Presentation of Christ which occurs halfway between the Winter Solstice and Spring Equinox.

Abiding refers to the Bible verse Isaiah 61:1.

Some Care is for Craig Cones.

ABOUT THE AUTHOR

Lisa Rhoades holds an MFA in Writing from Columbia University and Louisiana State University and is the author of three books of poetry. Her first, *Strange Gravity* was selected by Elaine Terranova as winner of the Bright Hill Press Poetry Award Series, and was published by Bright Hill Press in 2004. *The Long Grass* followed in 2020 and was published by Saint Julian Press. Her poems have appeared in *Calyx*, *Nimrod International Journal*, *Rust and Moth*, *The Southern Review*, *Tupelo Quarterly*, *West Trestle Review*, and many other journals.

Her awards and honors include Poetry Fellow at the Wisconsin Institute for Creative Writing, Writer in Residence at SWIMM—The Betsy South Beach and residency at The Virginia Center for the Creative Arts. A native of the Midwest, she lives in New York City on Staten Island with her spouse. Before becoming a nurse, she taught at CUNY College of Staten Island, Rutgers University, and as Visiting Poet through Poets and Writers Poetry in the Branches and the Geraldine R. Dodge Foundation. She is the mom of two fantastic people.

Visit her Amazon author page at: *amazon.com/author/lisarhoades* and follow her work at *http://lisarhoades.com*.

www.ingramcontent.com/pod-product-compliance
Lightning Source LLC
Chambersburg PA
CBHW021339060726

47591CB00006B/2101